Science Magic Tricks

by Nathan Shalit

SCIENCE MAGIC TRICKS

illustrated by
Helen Cerra Ulan

Holt, Rinehart and Winston
New York

Library of Congress Cataloging in Publication Data
Shalit, Nathan.   Science magic tricks.   Includes index.
Summary: Dozens of scientific "magic tricks"
based in mathematics, chemistry, optical illusion,
paper cutting, and magnetism.
    1. Science—Experiments—Juvenile literature.
[1. Scientific recreations. 2. Mathematical
recreations] I. Ulan, Helen Cerra. II. Title.
Q164.S47 793.8 79-18645 ISBN 0-03-047116-8

This book is dedicated to all
the bright-eyed, devious children
in the world who want to show
their friends how smart they are.

N.S.

Contents

Introduction   11

How to Be a Mathematical Genius   13
Magic Squares   13   /   Calendar Trick   15
Magic Addition Boxes   17   /   Subtraction Trick   19
Take a Number   20   /   Magic Numbers   21

Disappearing Squares and Lines   25
Magic Square   25   /   Magic Triangle   29
Magic Rectangle   29
Magic Envelope   30   /   Magic Hexagon   32

Chemistry Tricks   33
Before You Begin   33   /   Magic Flower   34
Deep Purple Magic   37   /   Magic Tea Glass   38
Witch's Dust   38   /   Secret Writing   41
More Secret Writing - Magic Candle   42
Magic Wet Fire   43   /   Red, White, and Blue   44
Magic Ketchup   45   /   Magic Ink   47
Magic Green Flame - 1   48
Magic Green Flame - 2   48

Tricks with Inertia   50
Energetic Coins   50   /   Tower of Discs   50
Spearing a Potato   51   /   Lazy Jar   51
Coin on a Card   51

Paper Cutting   53
Magic Star   53   /   Magic Paper Doorway   55
Paper Helicopter   57   /   The Monster Doll   58
Hex and Double Hex   61

Tricks with Magnets   65
Magic Boat   65   /   Magic Rings   67
Magic Jar #1   70

Don't Believe Your Eyes … Optical Illusions   72
Tunnel Flip-Flop   72   /   The Long and Short of It   73
Magic Boomerang   74
Magic Hexagon   76   /   Magic Box   76
Corinth Canal   78   /   The Impossible Fork   79
Magic Staircase   80   /   Magic Pile of Boxes   81

Tricks with Physics   82
Flying Ping-Pong Ball   82   /   Magic Pegboard   84
Magic Lung Power   87   /   Magic Glass Rod   88
Magic Comb   90   /   Magic Broomstick   92
Magic Mirror   93   /   Cutting Glass with a Scissors   94
Crumpled Can   96   /   Magic Harbor   98
Magic Jar #2   98

Miscellaneous Tricks 100
Paper Stretcher 100 / Magic Counting Block 101
Egg Magic 103 / Magic Peephole 104
Blind Spot 106 / Pin in a Balloon 107
Magic Dollar Bill 107 / Jacob's Ladder 109

*Where to Find the Chemicals and Ingredients
  Used in these Tricks* 113

Some Mail-Order Sources of Chemicals 116

Making and Using Certain Ingredients 117

Index 121

Introduction

This is a book of magic tricks based on science, not on sleight of hand or tricky deceptions. Most of the magic tricks depend on laws of science and can be explained in scientific terms.

One very important part of doing a trick is the story you tell as you go along. The idea is to keep your audience interested or amused all the time. Among magicians this talk is called the patter. Your patter can be anything that will amuse or divert them: nonsense talk, jokes, or even a fake "careful explanation." Whichever patter you choose, it must sound interesting and be entertaining. You will find sample patter in the book. They are only examples. Make up your own patter. You must be natural and tell it in your own words. Practice your patter the same as you practice the trick itself.

You are a magician whether your audience is just one friend in your kitchen, or a group at school or a club.

You should have a business card to impress them. Something like the one shown on the next page is easily made from 3-x-5 file cards.

For Spectacular Scientific
Tricks and Magic Show

Wendy Bendy

REASONABLE RATES

201-111-2222   NEW YORK CITY

How to Be a Mathematical Genius

MAGIC SQUARES

This box of numbers is a magic square. The numbers in any row, straight or diagonal, add up to 15.

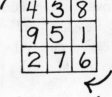

You can make it look different by turning the square like this.

Or using it in a mirror image, like this.
Memorize *one* of these magic squares.

To do your trick, draw an empty nine-box square on a blackboard or paper and ask your audience to call out numbers from 1 to 9 in any order. As they are called out, put them into the correct box. Of course, only *you* know where to put each number to make a magic square!

When all of the boxes are filled, ask your audience to add up the rows of numbers, and they will see that all the rows add up to 15.

11	4	9
6	8	10
7	12	5

Here is another square where the rows add up to 24. You can memorize this one too.

As above, ask your audience to call out numbers from 4 to 12. Write each number in the correct box of the square as it is called out. When the square is filled, ask your audience to add up the rows. Every row adds up to 24!

Your patter might go something like this: "When my mother was pregnant with me, she won a lot of money at a bingo game—enough to pay the doctor for my delivery. This made such an impression on her, that I was born with numbers buzzing through my head. Here is a square with nine empty boxes, etc."

If you *really* want to make an impression, here is a 25-box square where all the rows add up to 65! If you can memorize it, great. Otherwise you can write it on a tiny piece of paper and hide it in the palm of your hand with a bit of clear tape.

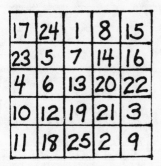

In this square, the horizontal, vertical and two long diagonal rows all add up to 65.

As before, draw your empty magic square on the blackboard and call for numbers from one to twenty-five in random order.

To further implant in the minds of your audience that you are indeed a wizard, repeat the performance, but in your mind first give the square a quarter turn or two and fill in the boxes accordingly. It will look like a completely different magic square which you are able to make to add up to 65 again.

CALENDAR TRICK

You can take any page of a calendar and mark off a square four numbers across and four numbers up and down. The sum of the numbers in the upper left and lower right corners will always equal the sum of the remaining two corners. In the illustration it is 36.

Do this: Circle any number inside the square and cross out all the other numbers in the same row across and

BOOKS FOR YOUNG READERS

S	M	T	W	T	F	S
					1	2	3
4	5	6	7	8	9	10
11	12	13	14	15	16	17
18	19	20	21	22	23	24
25	26	27	28	29	30	

HOLT, RINEHART AND WINSTON - PUBLISHERS

the same up-and-down row. Now circle a number you haven't marked yet and do the same thing. Continue until all the numbers in the marked square are either circled or crossed out. The sum of the circled numbers will be the same as the sum of the four corner numbers—in this case 72.

To do this trick, ask someone in your audience to mark off a 4-x-4 square on a calendar page while you watch. As this is done, be sure to see the numbers in either set of opposite corners. In your head, add them and multiply by two. Write the total on a piece of paper, fold it several times, and hand it to one of your audience for safekeeping.

Now tell the person holding the calendar page to hide it from your view and then to circle numbers and cross out, as described above. When all the numbers have been crossed out and circled, tell someone to add up all the circled numbers; then open your piece of paper, and show everyone that you had predicted the correct answer, in this case—72

Remember, you must be sure to see one set of corner numbers!

Your patter can go something like this: "I have magic telepathic perception which enables me to see into the immediate future. I am therefore able to foresee the numbers you will circle and know their total even before you circle them. There is no way you can squirm out of this situation, because I will have perceived it before you do it."

MAGIC ADDITION BOXES

This is a very easy trick to do. It is a trick where you show a square made of many boxes; each box has a number in it, as in the illustration, and is large enough for a penny to fit in it and cover the number.

Ask your audience to cover any number with a penny and cross out all the numbers in line with it in the rows across and down, just as in the Calendar Trick on page 15. Have them repeat this out of your sight until all the numbers are either covered or crossed out. Then announce the sum of all the covered numbers—in this case, 52. When the pennies are removed and the numbers added, everyone will see that you were right!

If you study the square in the illustration for a minute, you will see that it is really an addition square. Each number inside the square is really the sum of the two numbers outside the two rows—across and up and down—that number is in.

You can build such a square with any number of boxes. We chose to use a 5-x-5 square, and we chose 52 as our key number. Any two-digit number will work. First make the square. To make it easy to remember the key number for the square you have built, put the digits of the key number in the upper left and lower right boxes. In our illustration the 5 and the 2 are so placed. Then, in pencil, put numbers outside the square that add up to those digits—these numbers are circled in the illustration. The 2 plus the 3 equal the 5, and the 0 and 2 equal 2. Now write other numbers on the outside of the square in pencil. Any numbers will do, as long as they all add up to your key number—52 for this square. In our illustration we have

	②	8	6	9	⓪
③	5	11	9	12	3
10	12	18	16	19	10
7	9	15	13	16	7
5	7	13	11	14	5
②	4	10	8	11	2

chosen the 8, 6, and 9, and the 10, 7, and 5. Now fill in the boxes by adding up the outside numbers. The 8 and the 3 equal 11, 6 + 3 = 9, 9 + 3 = 12, 0 + 3 = 3. This completes the top row in our illustration. Complete the rest of the square. Now erase all the penciled numbers outside the square and you are ready for your trick. Prepare several such squares, each one different, so that your presentation will have variety and mystery.

SUBTRACTION TRICK

Tell your audience that you are not only a mathematical genius, but that you can also read their minds.

Tell someone to think of a three-digit number where the three digits are all different, reverse it, and subtract the smaller from the larger number. Let them use paper and pencil. Ask for the last digit of the answer, and then immediately announce the whole answer.

It's as easy as pie. When the smaller number is subtracted from the larger, the middle digit is always 9, and the two outside digits always add up to 9. So, given the last digit, you can quickly determine the first digit, and you know the middle one is 9, so you have the whole answer. Here's an example.

Number thought of	451
Reversed	−154
Subtracted	297

If the last number is a nine, the first must be a zero, since you know that the first and last number must add up to nine. The answer in such a case is 099.

TAKE A NUMBER

This is a "take-a-number" trick that is easy to do, yet mystifying. It is simple enough for your audience to do without pencil and paper. The variations are endless. You can change it each time you do it to keep your audience off balance.

Tell your audience to think of a number, triple it, add 18, divide by 3, subtract the original number. Tell them that the answer is 6. Several people can do it at once, and each may think of a different number, yet the answer will always be 6.

Variation: The "add" number can be any number divisible by 3. Then the answer will always be ⅓ of the "add" number.

Variation: Think of a number, double it, add 18, take the half (divide by 2), subtract the original number. The answer will be 9, which is half the "add" number.

How this works can be seen if you examine the process closely. You have taken a number and multiplied it by three and then divided it by three again (forgetting the added number for a moment). So you're back where you started, except for the added number. When you subtract the first number, what's left is nothing except a third of the added number. The number you multiply by must always be the same as the one you divide by, and the number you add must be an even multiple of it.

$$\frac{N \times 3 + 18}{3} - N = 6$$

MAGIC NUMBERS

The following pages describe a few magic numbers. They are all strange, and have strange things happen to them. You can have lots of fun with your friends if you memorize them and play with them.

Tell your audience that when you were very little you had several sets of blocks with numbers on them. You used to build castles and walls with them. Frequently, when they fell down, they were arranged in strange and magic combinations. Following are some.

Pass out paper and pencil and tell your audience to add, and then to multiply, the following pairs of numbers: 9 and 9, 24 and 3, 47 and 2, 497 and 2. Tell them to examine their answers and see the magic relationships between the answers. The addition answers and the multiplication answers have their digits reversed.

$$9 + 9 = 18 \qquad 9 \times 9 = 81$$
$$24 + 3 = 27 \qquad 24 \times 3 = 72$$
$$47 + 2 = 49 \qquad 47 \times 2 = 94$$
$$497 + 2 = 499 \qquad 497 \times 2 = 994$$

This magic number is 37.

Ask your audience to multiply this number by 1, by 2,

by 3, etc., through 9. Then multiply each answer by 3, and see the magic sequence of answers.

The answers will be 111, 222, 333, 444, etc.

This magic number is 12345679. Notice there is no 8 in it.

Tell your audience to multiply this number by 1, 2, 3, 4, etc. Then, since nine is the largest digit and also has magic properties, tell them to multiply the answers by nine. They will be astounded by their answers. The answers will by 111111111, 222222222, 333333333, 444444444, etc.

Another magic number is 15873. Tell them that this time instead of 9, you will use the magic number, 7. Why is 7 magic? Well, there are 7 openings in the head, 7 days of the week; the sum of opposite faces of dice is 7, the Biblical span of life is 7 × 10. Tell them to multiply the number by 1, 2, 3, 4, etc., and then multiply the answers by 7.

The answers will be 111111, 222222, 333333, 444444, etc.

Now tell your audience to take the strings of ones, twos, threes, etc. and multiply each string by nine and see the magic results. Tell them to note the sum of the first and last digit of these answers.

Magic Number 142857

Pass out pencil and paper and ask each person, in turn, to multiply this number by 2, 3, 4, 5, and 6. Tell the next three people, if there are that many, to multiply it by 7, 14, and 21 respectively.

When the answers are ready, tell your audience to add the digits up in their answers. Each person will get the same total, 27, except the last three. They will get twice 27, or 54.

Next point out other magic features of the number. The first digits of all the answers are in ascending order, which you would expect since the number gets bigger as you multiply by a larger number. But all those first digits are contained in the magic number itself! All this is shown in the chart.

The next magic feature of this number is that all the answers have all the same digits in the same order as the original number! If you arrange them in a circle, you can see this magic fact.

Your patter might go something like this: "Once in a dream I saw a large truck go by. It had these numbers on its wheels: 1, 4, 2, 8, 5, 7, and they were going round and round. It made me dizzy, and when I awoke they were still going around in my head, so I wrote them down in a circle and found that they made a really magic number. See all the things it can do?"

$$142857 \times 1 = 142857 \text{ These digits added} = 27$$
$$\text{"} \quad \times 2 = 285714 \quad \text{"} \quad \text{"} \quad \text{"} \quad = 27$$
$$\text{"} \quad \times 3 = 428571 \quad \text{"} \quad \text{"} \quad \text{"} \quad = 27$$
$$\text{"} \quad \times 4 = 571428 \quad \text{"} \quad \text{"} \quad \text{"} \quad = 27$$
$$\text{"} \quad \times 5 = 714285 \quad \text{"} \quad \text{"} \quad \text{"} \quad = 27$$
$$\text{"} \quad \times 6 = 857142 \quad \text{"} \quad \text{"} \quad \text{"} \quad = 27$$

Now, if you multiply the magic number by multipliers larger than 6 you will see an interesting phenomenon. When the number is multiplied by 7, the answer is a string of 9's. When the number is multiplied by multiples of 7—14, 21, 28, etc.—the answer is also a string of 9's except that the first and last digits add up to 9.

But when the number is multiplied by other multipliers, as shown, the answers still show the original magic number with the digits in the same order, except that one of the digits is broken into two numbers and equals the sum of those numbers. For instance, when the number is multiplied by 8, the answer in the wheel is 1, 4, 2, 8, 5, 7 (6 + 1).

$$142857 \times 7 = 999999$$
$$8 = 1142856 \qquad 6 + 1 = 7$$
$$9 = 1285713 \qquad 3 + 1 = 4$$
$$10 = 1428570$$
$$11 = 1571427 \qquad 1 + 7 = 8$$
$$12 = 1714284 \qquad 1 + 4 = 5$$
$$13 = 1857141 \qquad 1 + 1 = 2$$
$$14 = 1999998 \qquad 1 + 8 = 9$$

Disappearing Squares and Lines

MAGIC SQUARE

The first trick in this group is one in which squares mysteriously appear and disappear.

Buy some graph paper at a stationery counter and rule off half- or one-inch squares into a large 8-x-8 square as shown in illustration A. Cut this into four pieces as shown.

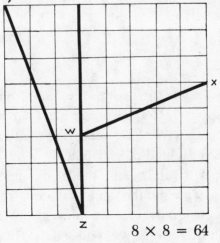

$8 \times 8 = 64$

Illustration A

Your presentation might go something like this. Show the 8-x-8 square and tell your audience, "Here is a magic block with 64 squares. Count them. Eight times eight equals sixty-four. This was purchased from a German mathematical genius who later died without revealing its secret. A square comes and goes, appears and disappears, and no one knows why. We must await the arrival of another Einstein to explain the mystery. In the meantime, let me show you what happens. Watch."

Rearrange the four pieces as shown in B, and let your audience see that you now have an extra, or 65, squares: $5 \times 13 = 65$.

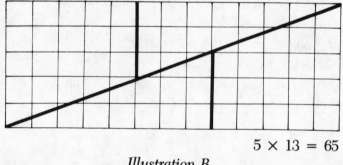

$$5 \times 13 = 65$$

Illustration B

Again rearrange the pieces, this time as in C. Now a square disappears. The two larger blocks are each 5×6, or 30. This makes twice 30, or 60, plus the three connecting squares for a total of only 63!

These tricks work because the small angles of the triangular pieces are not the same as the small angles of the four-sided pieces. If you examine the original 8-x-8 square in illustration A, you will see that line WX takes

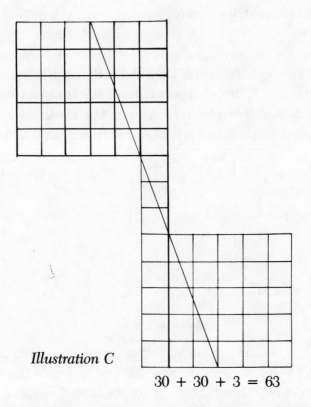

Illustration C

$$30 + 30 + 3 = 63$$

exactly five squares to move up two squares, while the line YZ takes a little *more* than five squares to move up two squares.

If you make the trick out of stiff paper and carefully try to put it together in the rearranged forms, being careful to line up the vertical and horizontal lines, you will see that they really don't fit well—there are spaces between the pieces. So using the flimsier paper will cover up the bad fit. If anyone remarks about this, you can say, "I guess my cuts weren't exactly straight."

The second trick in this group involves a disappearing line.

Draw a rectangle on a piece of paper or cardboard, and draw one diagonal. Then draw thirteen lines as in illustration D, being sure that the lines are exactly the same distance apart from each other. Use a ruler. Be sure, also, that the first and last lines just touch the diagonal.

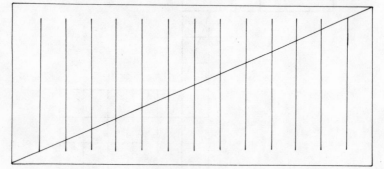

Illustration D

Now cut out the rectangle, and cut it along the diagonal so that you have two triangles. When you slide the triangles as in illustration E, one of the lines disappears!

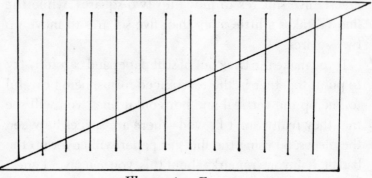

Illustration E

Tell your audience that since 13 is not a lucky number, you are going to make one vanish so that you end up with a neater dozen lines.

This trick works because, though you always end up with one line less than you started with, each line is just a little bit longer than it was originally.

MAGIC TRIANGLE

You will need paper, pencil, ruler, and scissors.

Tell one of your audience to draw a triangle, using the ruler, and then to cut it out. Mark the corners: 1, 2, and 3. Tell them that this is now a magic triangle. Tear or cut off the three corners and rearrange them as shown to form a straight line. You can repeat this with any triangle. It always forms a straight line.

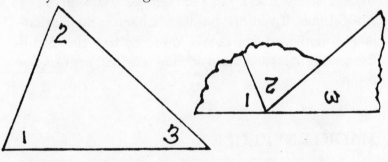

MAGIC RECTANGLE

You will need paper, pencil, ruler, compass, and scissors.

Tell your audience to draw a square or rectangle or any four-sided figure. Use the ruler. It need not be even, as long as the sides are straight. With compass, draw an arc—a partial circle—on each corner of the rectangle without changing the compass. Cut out the rectangle, then cut off the corners and rearrange them as shown. The arcs will form a perfect circle.

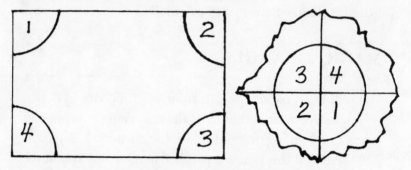

These two tricks work because they follow a basic rule of plane geometry. This is that the three inside angles of a triangle always add up to 180 degrees. 180 degrees is a straight line. If you draw a diagonal across a quadrilateral—a four-sided figure—you form two triangles. So all the inside angles add up to 360 degrees. 360 degrees is a complete circle.

MAGIC ENVELOPE

You will need something with which to draw a circle—a compass or small saucer. You will also need paper, pencil, and an ordinary envelope.

Tell your audience that you have a magic envelope. It is magic because the post office delivered it on time. Tell them it is magic because with it you can divide a circle exactly in half and find the exact center of the circle.

Draw a circle on a piece of paper.

Place the envelope on the circle so that one corner just touches the inside of the circle. Make a mark at the two places where the sides of the envelope cross the circle. Using the envelope as a ruler, connect these two points. This line, called a diameter, divides the circle exactly in half. Do this again with the same circle from a different position. The point where the diameters cross is the center of the circle.

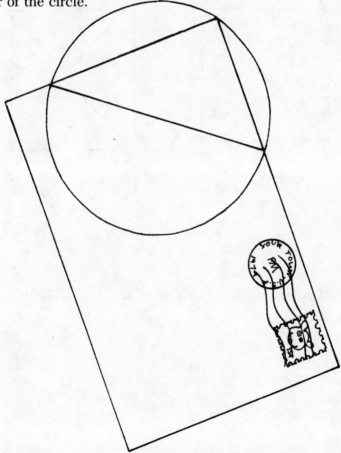

MAGIC HEXAGON

Ask your audience if anyone can draw the figure in the first illustration without retracing or crossing a line.

The way to do it is shown in the second illustration.

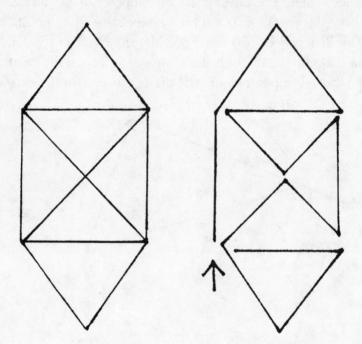

Chemistry Tricks

BEFORE YOU BEGIN

Note: All the tricks described in this part of the book are harmless and perfectly safe to do. However, several of the chemicals can be harmful if misused. Therefore, you must follow the directions and do the tricks only as instructed. Do not experiment with them beyond the directions given here unless you are supervised by an adult who has had training in chemistry.

All the chemicals are easily rinsed off with water. The oils, paint thinner, and phenolphthalein solution need a little extra washing with soap. When washing phenolphthalein off your hands with soap, the suds will turn pink. When you have finished each trick, carefully throw away all the used material and clean all your utensils.

Do not taste any chemicals. Be careful not to get any into your eyes.

Do not inhale ammonia (other than that which escapes into the air while you are doing a trick).

When doing any trick with fire, have a jar or pitcher of water handy to use as a fire extinguisher, in case of need. Protect the desk or tabletop with a cookie tin or some other suitable item.

When using iodine, protect the tabletop with a thick batch of newspaper, placing a layer of aluminum foil in between one of the layers of paper.

Finally, do the trick exactly as instructed and you will have no trouble. You will have only FUN.

At the back of the book, you will find a listing of all the chemicals used for these tricks, where to get them or how to make them easily, and how to use them safely.

MAGIC FLOWER

This is a dramatic trick which you must prepare ahead of time. You will need Q-tips, tincture of iodine, concentrated cabbage water, phenolphthalein solution, copper sulfate solution, turmeric solution, ammonia solution, water in a small glass, ball-point pen, and typing paper.

On a sheet of typing paper make a simple outline drawing of a flower, sun, and sunrays using a ball-point pen. (Do not use felt-tip or fountain pens, as the ink will run.) Make it large, something like the illustration. Using the Q-tips as paintbrushes, a different one for each "color," fill in the ball of the sun and the sunrays with the turmeric solution, and the center of the flower with the copper sulfate solution. Paint the petals with the phenolphthalein solution, and the stem and leaves with the concentrated cabbage water. When the picture is dry, the sun, sunrays, center of the flower, and the leaves and stem should each be a faint color. The petals will be colorless.

You are also going to paint clouds and raindrops. The paint for this is an iodine solution. To prepare this, put enough tincture of iodine into a little water to make it look like strong tea. (See page 34 for tips on using iodine safely.) But the clouds and raindrops are painted in *only* at the time you do your trick. You can do this as you tell your story.

To do the trick, you might start with a story like this: You were out early on a misty spring morning and were disappointed because the day was damp and gray. Nevertheless you picked a flower, the first flower of spring. Show your picture of the flower and tell them that is the way it looked to you. Tell them that later the sun came out, dried up the rain, and brightened the flower. At this point, wet a paper towel with the ammonia solution, and wipe it across the picture. The sun and sunrays will brighten up into a deep warm orange color, the clouds and raindrops will disappear, and the flower will bloom in bright colors: red petals, blue center, and green stem and leaves.

This trick works because the cabbage water, turmeric, and phenolphthalein are what chemists call indicators. They indicate the presence of an alkali, or base, by changing color. Ammonia is an alkali, so it turns the phenolphthalein pink, the cabbage green, and the turmeric a dark orange color.

Ammonia forms a dark blue compound with copper sulfate.

Iodine and starch form a blue compound when mixed. Most writing and typing paper has starch in it to make it smooth. So when you paint clouds and rain on the paper with iodine, the drawing appears blue. Before your performance try out a sample of your paper to be sure this will work. Ammonia forms a colorless compound with iodine, so that when you wipe ammonia across the picture, the blue clouds and rain disappear.

DEEP PURPLE MAGIC

This is a quick, fascinating trick. You will need a few clear (not colored) glass bottles or jars—baby food jars are good—a bottle of tincture of iodine, and some mineral oil, baby oil, or paint thinner (mineral spirits or "subturps").

Fill a bottle about half full of water and add enough iodine to make it the color of tea. Hold it up so everyone can see the amber-colored water. Slowly add some of the oil and hold it up again so everyone can see the clear oil floating on the water. Tighten the cap and shake the bottle hard for a half minute.

While shaking, tell them that you are going to transfer the iodine from the water to the oil, and for good measure you will change the color from amber to purple.

When you are through shaking, stand the bottle where everyone can see it. They will see the two layers slowly separate. The bottom layer will be much lighter in color, and the upper layer will be a beautiful purple color.

This trick works because iodine really is purple, not brown. It is brown in tincture of iodine because of a chemical trick to make it soluble in water. Iodine is naturally soluble in oils, where it shows its true color. In this trick we demonstrate this fact. When we shake hard and mix the oil and the water, the iodine moves from the water into the oil.

MAGIC TEA GLASS

In this trick you will turn "tea" into "water." You must have a clear glass pitcher of water into which you put enough tincture of iodine to color it a nice amber tea color. Into a clear drinking glass put several crystals of sodium thiosulfate (photographers' hypo), and a tea-spoonful of water. When you pour the "tea" into the apparently empty glass, the amber color will disappear, and the "tea" will seem to have changed to "water."

Your patter might go something like this: "I have a Chinese friend who drinks an awful lot of tea. I am going to play a trick on him. I am going to give him a gift of a magic glass like this one, and when he pours tea into it, the tea will change to water." At this point pour the "tea" from the pitcher into the glass. You can emphasize the trick by repeating it. Pour most, but not all, of the liquid from the glass. There should be enough hypo left in it so that you can pour again from the pitcher and have the liquid lose its amber color. Work this out well before you try it in front of an audience.

This trick works because hypo forms a colorless chemical compound with iodine.

WITCH'S DUST

You will need several sugar cubes, matches, a saucer, and a small quantity of cigarette ashes.

To do your trick, put a sugar cube in a dish and ask one of your audience to set it afire with the matches. They can try again and again, but the sugar will not burn. It will sizzle and melt, but it won't burn. Then you tell this story:

"I have here a jar of certified genuine witch's dust. I know that it is genuine, because it was given to me last Halloween by a real witch. It is made from the scraping from the bottom of her kettle after she made her brew of toads, lizards, and weird things like that. It is dried and ground into this powder. The witches use it to draw fire—lightning—from the sky to start their fires. I will show you how efficient it is."

Then rub a small amount of the ashes on a fresh sugar cube and say some magic sentence, like "Dust of bones and witch's attire, I command you to draw some fire." Put a lighted match to the sugar cube. It will start to burn with a nice blue flame.

The sugar burns after you put some cigarette ashes on it because the ashes act as a catalyst. In chemistry, a catalyst is something that starts or helps along a chemical reaction without itself being changed. Catalysts are important in many chemical industries, and are widely used in oil refining.

You can expand on the magic power of the witch's dust as follows: Before the demonstration, out of sight of anyone, write the word HEX on the back of your hand with a piece of wet soap. After the fire trick is done, tell your audience that you are going to brand yourself with the powder left over from the fire. Sprinkle some on the back of your hand and pat it down. Wince and make faces as you do it, as if it were painful. Then show your hand. The word HEX will be visible where the powder sticks to the soaped skin.

If you have a sink or a large pan of water handy, you can continue with the following. You must have prepared for this by painting some phenolphthalein solution on your hand and allowing it to dry.

After you have displayed the HEX on the back of your hand, tell your audience that you were really branded. You will wash off the dust and blood. Wash your hands with a bar of soap; the soapy water will turn bright red. Show the audience how much "blood" there was. After you have cleaned up, and the back of your hand shows no scars or damage, you can say, "Oh well, magic is magic, and with my magic powers I have healed my hand so you cannot see where it was branded."

This trick works because soap is made from fat plus a strong alkali boiled together to form the chemical compound we call soap. When water is added, some of this compound breaks down so that there is some free alkali in the solution, hence the red color with phenolphthalein. That is why some soaps are more irritating to your skin than others. It depends on how much of the alkali is freed in the solution.

SECRET WRITING

For this trick you will need phenolphthalein solution, ammonia, tincture of iodine, a few Q-tips, paper towels, and typing paper. Mix some of the ammonia half and half with water.

On a sheet of white paper, using the Q-tip as a pen, write the word SUMMER with the phenolphthalein solution as the ink. Allow it to dry thoroughly. The writing will be invisible.

Into a small jar with a little water in it, pour enough of the iodine to make it look like tea. Almost all writing paper has starch in it, and when you write on it with a Q-tip using the iodine as an ink, the writing appears blue. Before your performance, check a sample of your paper to be sure this will occur.

To do your trick, tell a story of how it takes three months to go from winter to summer. But after a few cold months you are in a hurry for summer, and can't wait. So you will turn winter into summer in a few seconds. At this point write the word WINTER with the iodine solution. It will be in blue letters. Wet a paper towel with the diluted ammonia and wipe it across the word WINTER. The word will disappear, and in its place will appear the word SUMMER in bright pink. When the ammonia evaporates, the word will disappear. But it can be brought back again with more ammonia.

You can change BLUE to RED, circles to squares, or anything your imagination comes up with.

The reason this works is explained on page 36.

MORE SECRET WRITING—MAGIC CANDLE

This is a trick where you write a secret message with a magic candle, and make the writing visible with some magic tea. You will need sheets of paper, a candle, some tincture of iodine, a jar of water, paper towels, and some old newspapers.

Prepare your "magic tea" ahead of time. Put ten or twenty drops of the iodine into a small jar of water so that it looks like tea.

Write the invisible message on a sheet of paper using a candle as a pen. Any candle will do. Use ordinary pressure on the paper. Lay the sheet on a table that is protected by several layers of newspaper. Wipe the sheet

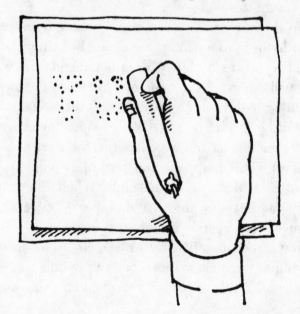

with a paper towel soaked with the "magic tea." The sheet will turn blue, and the message will remain white and clearly readable.

The reason this works is that the paper contains starch, and it turns blue in contact with iodine. But the candle wax prevents the iodine from touching the places where you have written.

You might tell some story that the magic candle was made with tallow from the sacred cows of India, and the tea is also imported from India.

MAGIC WET FIRE

This is a dramatic trick where you show a piece of cloth completely in flames, yet it is not destroyed. You will first need a piece of cloth. Half of an old handkerchief will do fine. You will also need pliers or tongs to hold it, rubbing alcohol (70% *ethyl* alcohol) from the drugstore, a dishpan with some water in it, matches, and a pitcher of water to use as a fire extinguisher in an emergency.

The fuel used in this trick is made of two parts ethyl rubbing alcohol and one part water. To make it, put one cup of alcohol and one-half cup of water into a jar. Use your mother's measuring cups for accuracy. Rinse the measuring cups. Label the jar so that you know what it is the next time you need it. Do not store it where someone might accidentally drink it! Be sure to label it, "rubbing alcohol fuel."

While you are doing the trick, burning alcohol will

drip from the cloth. This must be caught in the pan of water, where it will immediately be extinguished.

Your patter might go something like this: "Here is a jar of magic fuel. It can burn itself, but won't ignite anything else. As soon as I work out a few details, I am going to sell it to the utility company for use as a household fuel. While you could cook with it and heat your house, there is no danger of burning down the house. I will demonstrate."

This trick works because there is too much water in the fuel to sustain the fire. When you mix the alcohol with the water your resulting fuel is 50%, or half, pure alcohol. As soon as enough of the alcohol burns off so that it drops below 50%, or half, the excess water puts out the fire.

RED, WHITE, AND BLUE

This is a nice Fourth of July trick. In this trick you fill three glasses from a pitcher that seems to contain only water. The first glassful turns red, the second white, and the last blue. You will need a pitcher, ammonia, phenolphthalein solution, epsom salts, and copper sulfate.

Put a half inch of water into each glass. Into the first put five or more drops of phenolphthalein solution. Into the second put about a teaspoonful of epsom salts, and into the third put a quarter teaspoonful or less of copper sulfate. Swish the glasses around until the chemicals are dissolved. Line up the three glasses on a table. It might be a good idea to put some books on the table in front of the glasses to hide the liquid in the bottoms of the glasses. Hold up each glass, covering up the bottom part with your fingers. Tell your audience that you will fill these glasses from a magic pitcher which is in tune with the holiday. The liquid in the pitcher should be half ammonia and half water.

Fill the glasses from the pitcher.

This works because the phenolphthalein is an indicator; it turns red in the presence of an alkali, as explained on page 36. The copper sulfate forms a deep blue substance with ammonia. The epsom salts and magnesium sulfate—when mixed with an alkali—form a heavy white substance, magnesium hydroxide. This is an impure form of milk of magnesia.

MAGIC KETCHUP

In this trick you write a word on the bottom of a copper-clad frying pan with ketchup.

You will need a copper-bottomed pan, ketchup, and some paper towels. To prepare for this trick, heat the pan dry on the stove so that the bottom turns all colors. Allow it to get cold so you don't burn yourself. The best way to handle the ketchup is with a plastic squeeze dispenser with a pointed nozzle.

To do the trick, all you have to do is write a word on the bottom of the pan with ketchup. You might even lick some off your fingers to show how pure it is. Leave the pan alone while you tell your story. After two or three

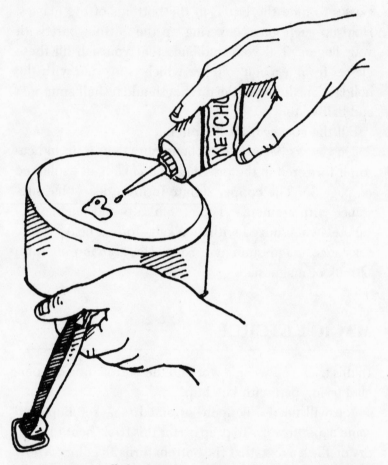

minutes wipe off the ketchup with a damp paper towel. The word you wrote will appear in bright shiny copper. Do not eat any of the ketchup after it has been on the copper pan. You can ask your audience to count the time for the two or three minutes. This will keep them more interested in waiting for the outcome.

You might tell your audience that the trick was taught

to you by your grandmother. She didn't want you to eat so much ketchup so she told you, "Look what it does to my copper pans. What will it do to your stomach?"

The trick works because ketchup contains salt and vinegar, an acid. These two ingredients combine with the tarnish, and leave the bright copper.

When you have finished, wash the pan well before putting it away so there won't be any dried-up ketchup on it to burn when it is used for cooking.

MAGIC INK

Prepare three glasses which will look empty. Into the first put a few specks of tannin, into the second a few drops of ferric chloride, and into the third a few crystals of oxalic acid. Put a half teaspoonful of water into each to dissolve the chemicals before you start.

Fill the first glass half full with water. It will look like pure water. Pour this into the second glass. It will turn dark blue or black, like ink. Pour this "ink" into the third glass. It will become decolorized and look like water again. Then pour this into the sink.

This works because ferric chloride, which is an iron salt, forms a dark blue substance with tannin. The oxalic acid forms a colorless, soluble substance with iron, so it "bleaches" the dark "ink." Old-fashioned liquid blue inks were iron-tannin mixtures.

MAGIC GREEN FLAME–1

You will need an empty soda can, a saucer, matches, methanol or Sterno, and some boric acid. You should also have a pitcher of water handy to use as a fire extinguisher if needed.

Do this trick in a darkened room. Into the hollow of the upside-down can, which sits in a saucer, put a small quantity of the Sterno or methanol and light it. It will burn with an almost invisible blue flame. Then sprinkle some of the boric acid over the flame, and it will change to a beautiful green flame.

You can tell your audience that you have some volcanic dust from the green island of Hawaii, and that it has the power to change a flame from blue to green.

This works because boric acid contains the element boron. Boron burns with a green flame.

MAGIC GREEN FLAME–2

Here is a simple green-flame trick. You will need a piece of old *copper* screening, a candle, and some long wooden kitchen matches.

Light the candle and hold the screen in the flame. None of the flame will go through the screen, but some of the smoke will. Hold a lighted match in the stream of smoke. The match flame will burn with green edges.

You can tell your audience that you have a magic

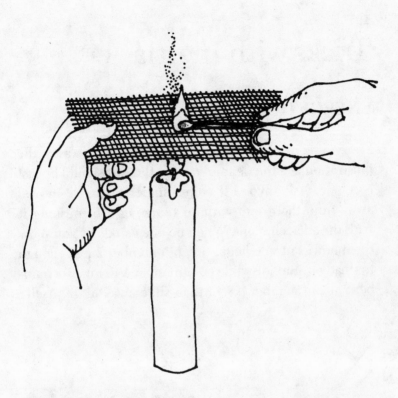

screen and magic candle, the same as described on page 42. Tell them that the magic screen filters out the yellow light and lets the true green flame through. Your trick will be more effective if you use a green candle.

This works because some copper from the screen goes into the hot candle smoke as gas. The match ignites this gas and the copper burns with a green flame. Scientific instruments can show that this is a different green from the green of the boron flame.

Tricks with Inertia

ENERGETIC COINS

Line up six or more pennies on a table or desk as in the illustration. All the pennies except the first should be just touching. Ask anyone if coin number 8 can be moved away from the group without touching it or pushing it with the adjacent coin. When no one can do it, you show them how. Put one finger on coin number 2 just enough to steady it. Rapidly slide coin number 1 to hit coin number 2. Coin number 8 will then slide away all by itself.

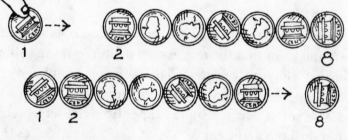

TOWER OF DISCS

Another trick is done with a stack of checkers. Ask anyone to remove the bottom checker without disturbing the rest of the pile. It's easy. Slide a table knife rapidly along the table to knock out the bottom checker. The rest will settle down on the table without falling over.

SPEARING A POTATO

You will need a raw potato and several plastic soda straws.

Ask anyone in your audience to push the straw through the potato. Let them try. As they push, the straw will only bend. Everyone will fail.

Then you do it.

Thrust the straw very quickly with one fast strong thrust right into and through the potato.

LAZY JAR

Place a jar of jam, or any such heavy object near the edge of a sheet of paper, and ask someone to remove the paper without moving the jar. It's easy. Grasp the paper tightly and yank it out with one strong sudden pull.

If anyone is able to do any of these tricks before you demonstrate how, don't be flustered. Just congratulate him or her. Tell them they must be fellow witches to have the magic touch, and go rapidly on to your next trick.

COIN ON A CARD

This is a neat, fast trick. You will need a coin and a small piece of stiff paper. A half of a 3-x-5 file card will do fine.

Balance the card on your fingertip with a coin in the middle. Ask your audience if anyone can remove the card without moving the coin. If no one knows how, you tell them.

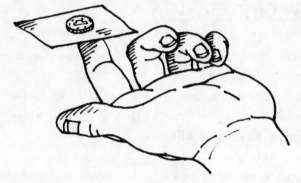

Tell them that you have a great attraction for money and that the coin will stick to your finger. Then with the fingers of your other hand, flick the edge of the card. It will fly away, and the coin will remain balanced on your finger. Practice this.

These tricks work because things at rest—not moving—like to stay at rest. They resist being put into motion. This is called inertia. So when you pull the paper from under the heavy jar, the paper is out and away before the jar can be put into motion. The same situation exists with the coin on your fingertip, and the pile of checkers. The plastic straw is relatively sharp and moves so rapidly it cuts through the potato before it bends.

The sliding penny trick is a bit different. The energy of the first moving penny is transmitted through all the other pennies. The last penny stands alone so the energy it receives is used to move it away from the others.

Paper Cutting

MAGIC STAR

This is a trick where you fold a piece of paper and with one single straight cut produce a beautiful star. Two variations are shown. Your patter can be straightforward. Tell your audience that you graduated from kindergarten with the degree of Doctor of Paper Folding by demonstrating the following trick.

You will need a scissors, and a supply of 8½"-x-11" paper. Very thin paper, called onion skin, is best, but ordinary paper will do.

Holding the paper so the longer side is across, fold the sheet of paper in half from left to right as in illustration 1. Find point E, which is exactly halfway between A and B, by folding A to B and putting a small crease at E to mark the point. Open out that fold again; bring point C exactly to E and crease the paper. It should look like illustration 2.

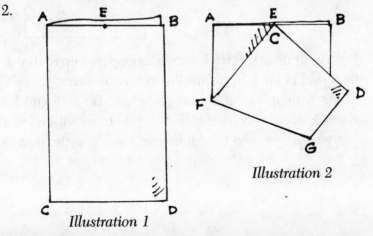

Illustration 1

Illustration 2

Fold A down along FE, crease the paper, and unfold it back flat. Bring G up past E to lay FG along the crease FE. Fold the paper and hold it in this position. It should look like illustration 3. Bring AF down on top of this by folding it where you creased it. The paper will now look like illustration 4. Cut the end off on the dotted line approximately as shown in illustration 4, and unfold both pieces to display the stars.

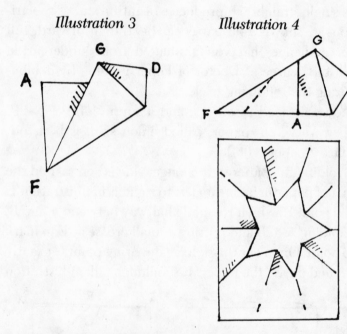

Illustration 3   *Illustration 4*

A variation of this trick is to fold the paper up to step 4, then fold point F up as in illustration 5 so that line FX makes a right, or square, angle with XH. X should be about ⅔ of the way from F to A. A few trials will tell you just where it should be. Make one cut along the dotted

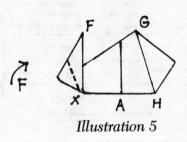

Illustration 5

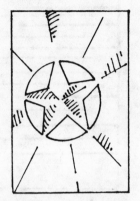

Illustration 6

line starting very close to but not quite at X. This cut should be parallel to GH. The resulting star, when the paper is unfolded, will look like illustration 6, a star in a circle.

MAGIC PAPER DOORWAY

This is a trick where a small piece of paper is cut in such a way that it can be spread out with a hole big enough for a person to step through.

Hold up half a sheet of paper and ask anyone if a hole can be cut in it big enough to walk through. When you are told it couldn't be done, you might answer something like this: "Do you think I would ask the question if I thought it couldn't be done?" Then show how to do it.

The paper must be cut so it looks like illustration B. This is best done by folding it in half and making the cuts as shown by the heavy lines in A. Cut from alternating sides to about a half inch from the opposite edge. The

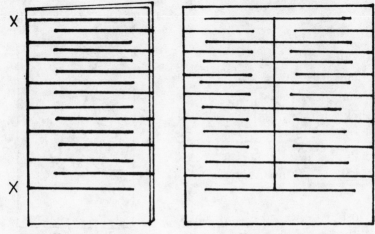

X		X

Illustration A   *Illustration B*

number of cuts you make is not important as long as the pattern is the same as the illustration. The more cuts you make, the thinner will be your strand of paper, and the larger the hole will be.

Then cut along the folded edge between the top cut and the bottom one, as between the X's in illustration A. If the sheet is now carefully unfolded, it will look like illustration B. Gently pull at the top and bottom of the sheet and you will have a large loop, similar to illustration C, that will be big enough for you to step through.

Illustration C

Try this at home a few times so you can decide how many cuts you can make without tearing the paper. If you have a sharp pair of scissors or an Exacto knife you can do this trick with an ordinary index card.

PAPER HELICOPTER

Most people know how to make a paper airplane or glider which will soar more or less successfully when thrown into the air. Ask your audience if anyone knows how to make a paper helicopter.

Here are the simple directions.

Start with a rectangle of paper and cut it as shown on the solid lines in A. Then fold on the dotted lines so you

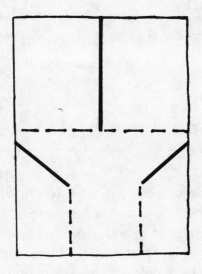

Illustration A

end up with the helicopter as shown in B. The bottom part is held together with several pieces of Scotch tape or a small paper clip. The wings are folded in opposite directions.

Hold it up over your head, and let go.

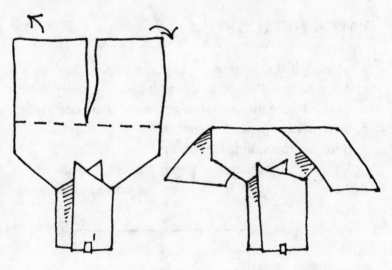

Illustration B

THE MONSTER DOLL

This is a trick where you fold a strip of paper into several accordion folds and cut out a paper doll. When the strip is unfolded, one of the dolls, mysteriously, has two heads!

You will need a good scissors and some strips of paper two to four inches wide. An adding machine roll is good. This can be bought at a stationery or office supply store.

You can make your own strips by cutting several sheets of paper lengthwise and sticking them together with Scotch tape.

The trick depends on the way the strip is folded and cut. Fold the strip into eight or nine 3″ accordion folds, but have one of the folds go only about a half inch past the center, as in illustration A. Make this half fold the

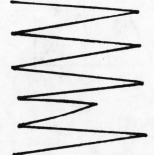

Illustration A

second or third fold, so that at the end of the trick the monster doll is just past the middle of the strip. The dotted lines in illustrations B, C, and D indicate the edge of the half fold.

Make the first cut as in B, almost to this edge. The second cut is the underside of the doll's arm. Then make the third cut as in C, a little past the folded edge. Then

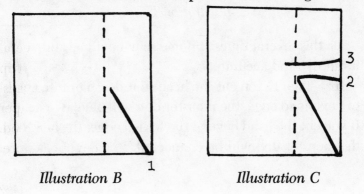

Illustration B 1   *Illustration C*

complete the cutout as in D. When unfolded, the strip will look like E.

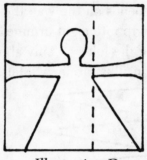

Illustration D

Illustration E

Do this several times at home so you will be able to do it quickly and accurately.

If at stage D you cut the head so it doesn't quite come to the folded edge, the monster doll will have two heads. If you cut the head beyond the folded edge, the heads on the monster doll will be connected.

HEX AND DOUBLE HEX

You will need a pen or pencil, scissors, Scotch tape, and a roll of adding machine tape or the paper tape that goes in a cash register. Your supermarket manager or any storekeeper can sell you a roll.

You must prepare several large loops of paper using strips about four feet long. Make one ordinary loop first. Then make a second loop, but give one end one twist before you tape it to the other end. Make a third loop giving one end two twists before taping the two ends together. If these loops are large enough your audience will probably not notice that there are twists in them. To do your trick, show the first loop and tell your audience that these are ordinary loops of paper and you are going to cut them in half lengthwise. Demonstrate on the first loop, and cut the entire length lengthwise until it falls apart into two loops.

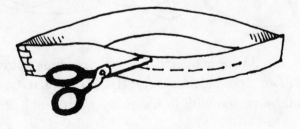

Now tell them that you are going to put a hex on one of the loops. Proceed to write HEX on the second loop. Tell your audience that it is now a magic loop. It is magic for two reasons. The paper is indestructible—it can't be cut in half—and it has only one side. To demonstrate, give one of your audience a pen and ask them to draw a line down the middle of the loop all the way around, being careful not to raise the pen from the paper. When the line is complete, hold up the loop and show that the line is on *both* sides of the paper, proving that there is really only *one* side to the paper.

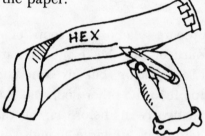

Now give another person the scissors and ask that the loop be cut in half by following the line made by the first person. When finished, the loop will not separate into two loops as expected, but will end up as one longer loop!

Next tell your audience that you are going to give the other loop a double hex. Write HEX HEX on it. Give this to a third person with instructions to cut it in half, care-

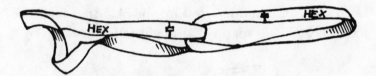

fully, down the middle. Won't they be surprised when they wind up with two separate but entwined loops!

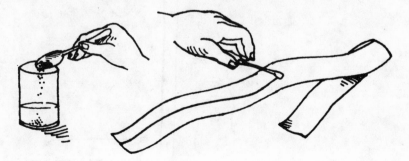

Here is a very dramatic variation of this trick. It should be done in a large room because it produces some smoke. You will need, in addition, some saltpeter (potassium nitrate) and a Q-tip. Put a teaspoonful of the saltpeter into a juice glass a quarter full of water and stir for a minute. Let it settle. With the Q-tip paint a heavy wet line with this solution down the middle of a long length of paper tape. Allow it to dry thoroughly. Make a loop with two twists and tape the ends together with two pieces of Scotch tape, one piece on either side of the center.

Hang the loop from a wire coat hanger so that it hangs free and the taped part is on top. Ignite the bottom center of the loop with a match, being careful that the loop does not catch fire but merely smolders in a red line. Leave it alone, watch the two red lines climb the paper loop, one up each side. When they meet at the top, the paper will fall into two intertwined loops.

When you do this trick, be sure to have a jar of water ready to use as a fire extinguisher if needed, and keep a large sheet of aluminum foil or a cookie tin under the loop to catch any sparks that might fall.

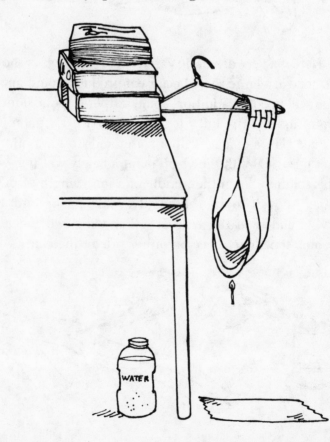

Tricks with Magnets

MAGIC BOAT

Make a small wooden boat three or four inches long. Just a simple piece of wood shaped like a hull will do fine. Ask an adult to help you bore a small hole in one end of the wood. Make it just big enough to hold a small straight magnet about an inch long. Push the magnet into the hole, stuff the hole so the magnet doesn't rattle, and seal and hide the hole by painting the boat.

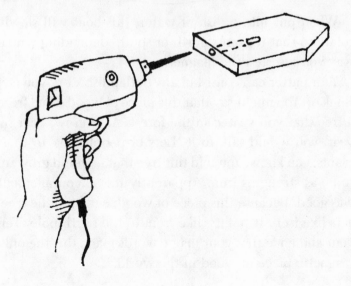

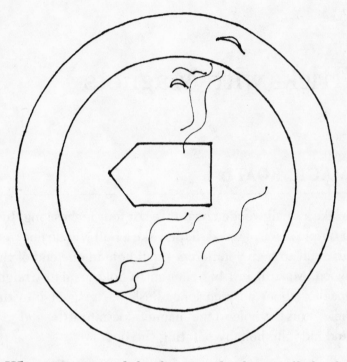

When put into a dish of water, this boat will slowly rotate so that it points north or south, depending which way you inserted the magnet.

Your patter can consist of any outlandish story you can think of. You might say that this piece of wood came from a tree that you visited in the forest. As it grew, year by year, you would talk to it. Lots of people talk to their plants, you know. You told this tree that it would grow up to be as strong as iron. Apparently this encouragement was good. Because this piece of wood, cut from the tree, acts like iron. It points, like iron, to the north pole. Tell your audience that your magic words made this the only magnetic piece of wood in the world.

MAGIC RINGS

You will need a wooden pencil or plastic ball-point pen and two or more ceramic ring magnets. These are special magnets and do not look at all like the common horseshoe magnets. Be sure that the magnets you get have their north and south poles on their *faces*, not on the edges. To make sure, test them. If they are right, they will first stick together, but when you turn one over, it will be repelled—it will not stick to the other magnet. To be doubly sure, take a pencil with you when you buy the magnets and try Trick Number 1. It must work if the magnets are correct.

Tell your audience that you have black rings that were made out in space near the planet Saturn, and were influenced by its rings.

Trick Number 1: Put two magnets on the pencil as shown, so that they repel each other. Hold the bottom ring and move it up and down along the pencil. The upper ring will jump up and down as if it were attached to a spring.

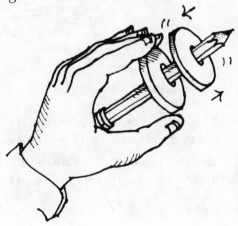

Trick Number 2: Put the magnets on a pencil as above, but this time hold the bottom ring and let go of the pencil. The pencil will stay put. It will not fall through the rings.

Trick Number 3: Lay one ring on the table, and set the second one near it, ¼" to ½" away as illustrated. Do this carefully and slowly to get it just right. The second magnet will vibrate standing only on one edge.

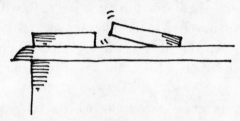

Trick Number 4: Hold two rings in the fingers of one hand as illustrated, about a quarter inch apart, so they repel each other. Hold tight to the bottom ring and loosen up on the upper ring. It will jump and flip over and stick to the first ring. This takes a little practice.

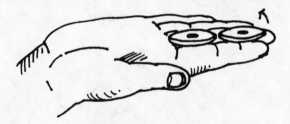

Trick Number 5: Hold one ring between your thumb and forefinger in a vertical position. Hang the second ring to it edge to edge. With a slight movement of your hand you can make the second ring travel round and round the

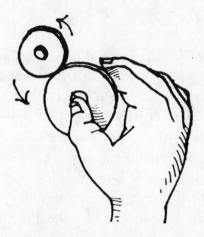

first ring. You can get more speed if the ring held in your hand is somewhat larger than the second one.

Trick Number 6: You will need a ring magnet, a sheet of paper, some iron filings, and salt, sugar, or sand.

Mix a half teaspoonful or so of sand (or sugar or salt) with a more or less equal quantity of iron filings on the sheet of paper. Ask your audience how to separate them. You may get several suggestions. Tell them you will separate the two with your magic Saturn ring. Hold the magnet under the paper, under the pile of sand-iron, and move it back and forth with a gentle sweeping movement. As you move the magnet, the iron filings will follow, but the sand will be left behind. Many repeated sweeping movements will get most of the iron separated from the sand.

If you held the magnet above the paper, the iron filings would cling to the magnet and be difficult to remove.

MAGIC JAR #1

In this trick an ordinary metal paper clip attached to a thread stands up in the air like a helium balloon.

You will need a glass jar with a metal screw cap similar to ones that olives or jelly come in, a large paper clip— about 2″—some thread, a piece of Scotch tape, and one or two of the ring magnets. You must ask your friendly dentist to drill a hole in the bottom of the jar for you.

Tie a length of thread to the paper clip. With the clip inside the jar, put the other end of the thread through the hole in the jar so that the clip hangs in the upside-down jar down to about ¾″ from the rim. Stick the thread to the bottom of the jar with a piece of tape. Put one or two ring magnets in the lid of the jar. They will stick by their own magnetism. You might wrap them in a bit of tissue

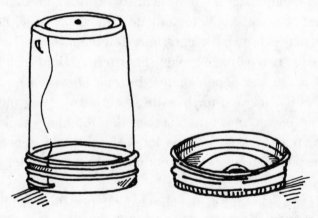

paper first, to hide them. Now turn the jar right side up and screw on the lid. The clip will be lying on the bottom of the jar.

Tell your audience that you have a magic jar. Tell them that it is filled with antigravitational space, and that a foreign country would like to know the secret so they can launch a space vehicle without the use of rockets.

At this point you turn the jar upside down. The clip will be strongly attracted to the magnet. Then carefully turn it right side up again. The clip will be suspended high in the jar, pulling on the thread and trying to go farther up, just like a miniature helium balloon.

Don't Believe Your Eyes...
Optical Illusions

The following tricks depend on the viewer's eyes telling him lies. Our eyes and brains sometimes play tricks on us, and things are not always what they seem to be. We will describe a few of these effects so you can use them as tricks to show your friends.

You might tell your audience that you will hypnotize them into seeing strange things. Say a few nonsense words and wave your hands in front of you. Tell them that they are in your power!

The next few are called flip-flops. As you look at them they seem to change from one point of view to another.

TUNNEL FLIP-FLOP

Tell a story. When the Holland Tunnel was built under the Hudson River, teams of workmen started on both sides of the river. They built strong rings of steel, one next to the other. They did this until they met in the middle, under the river. Here is a picture of rings. Look at it. Are you looking through it from New York to New Jersey, or from New Jersey to New York?

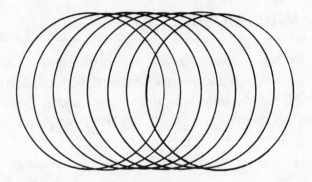

THE LONG AND SHORT OF IT

Show this drawing to your audience, and ask them to pick out the shorter and the longer lines. Ask them if any two lines are equal in length.

Line AB and BC are the same length.

You can make a similar drawing very easily. Draw lines AB and BC exactly the same length. Then connect A to C, and draw the other lines in somewhat the same shape as shown, putting point D way off to the right, so that the right part of the drawing is much larger than the left part. Now BC looks even longer than AB. This is a good illusion.

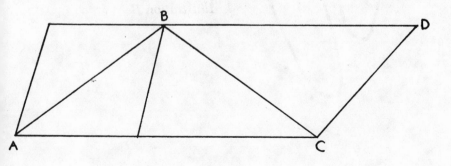

MAGIC BOOMERANG

Following are two sets of curved pieces. A looks smaller than B and 1 looks smaller than 2, but actually A and B are the same size and so are 1 and 2. Copy these and cut them out carefully. Reverse their positions, putting B above A and 2 above 1. Now their sizes seem to have been reversed too. The upper one always looks smaller.

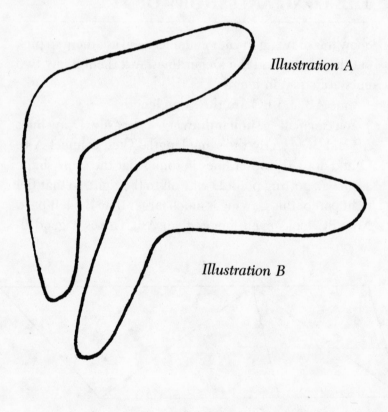

Illustration A

Illustration B

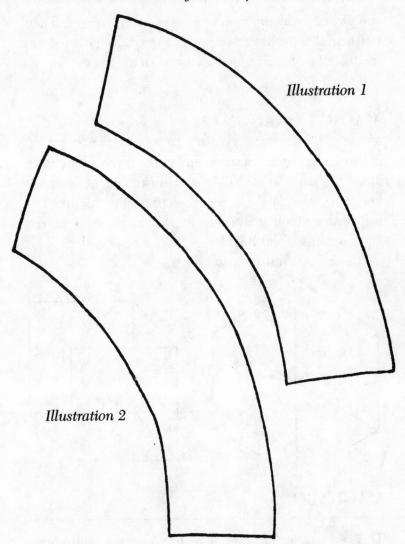

Illustration 1

Illustration 2

You might tell a story. Say that these are copies of Australian boomerangs which are now on display in natural history museums. When they are thrown into the air and picked up again, their sizes have been changed. Then lay them down in reversed positions so your audience can see that they have indeed changed size.

MAGIC HEXAGON

A regular hexagon is a six-sided figure where all the sides are of the same length. This is an illustration of a regular hexagon with straight lines connecting all the points. But is it? As you look at it, it flip-flops to an illustration of a cube, a transparent box. It becomes a box similar to the one in the illustration next to it.

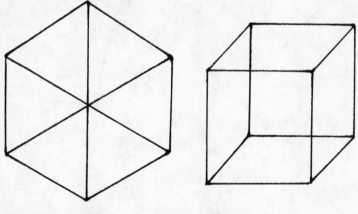

MAGIC BOX

This is a magic box similar to the one which flip-flops from the magic hexagon. As you look at this transparent box it flip-flops into any of the six boxes shown on the page.

The Magic Box

There seems to be no good explanation why these things flip-flop. Possibly the brain can see all the possibilities. But it can focus on only one at a time.

CORINTH CANAL

Two bridges cross a canal at different points. One is high, at ground level, and the other is low, at water level.

Is the AB bridge shorter or longer than the CD bridge? Try to guess and then measure each bridge.

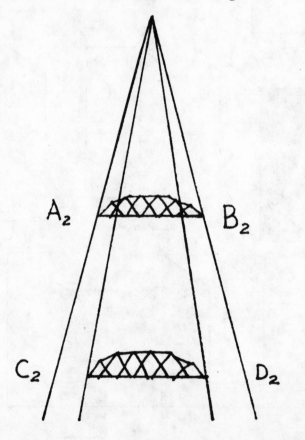

THE IMPOSSIBLE FORK

This is an impossible fork because you can't eat with it. Nobody can make one. In fact, you can hardly look at it without getting dizzy.

If you hide the tips of the prongs with your fingers, you will see *two* prongs. If you hold your fingers over the base of the prongs you will see *three* prongs.

Tell your audience that when they get dizzy looking at it, they should lie down and close their eyes.

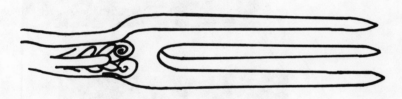

MAGIC STAIRCASE

This is another flip-flop illusion. The staircase first seems to be normal, going up to the right. As you look at it, it seems to flop and turn upside down.

You might tell a story of people trying to build a stairway into the sky. But they were never successful. As they climbed up, the staircase would flip over and they would fall off.

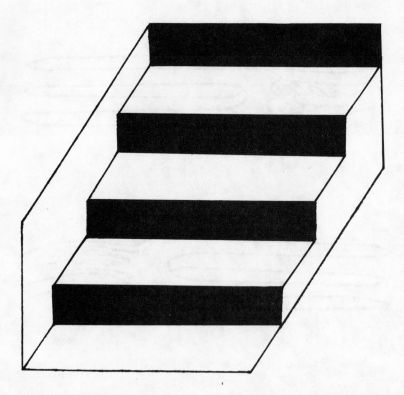

MAGIC PILE OF BOXES

This is a famous illusion which is frequently used to illustrate flip-flops.

As you look at it you sometimes see eight blocks; and sometimes, as you stare, it changes to seven blocks. Apparently our brains can handle only one view at a time, just as in the tunnel and other flip-flops shown in this book.

Tricks with Physics

FLYING PING-PONG BALL

In this trick you keep a Ping-Pong ball suspended in mid-air. You will need a hand-held hair dryer or a vacuum cleaner with a hose that can be attached so that it blows air out instead of sucking it in. You will also need one or more Ping-Pong balls.

Turn on the dryer or vacuum cleaner and hold it so that it blows straight up. Drop a Ping-Pong ball into the center of the stream of air. A low-power stream of air will work better than a more powerful stream. The ball will dance around suspended in the air. With a little practice you will be able to move it around the room without having it fall down.

This trick works because the stream of air going over a curved surface produces an area of lower pressure, pulling the object in the direction of the lower pressure. This is part of what is known as Bernoulli's Principle, and is part of the explanation of how airplane wings get their lift. Since the ball is round, not wing shaped, the lower pressure is all around so the ball stands approximately still.

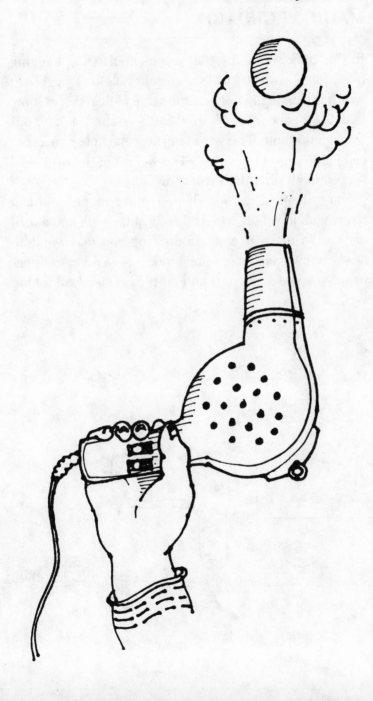

MAGIC PEGBOARD

In this trick you show that a weighted string hanging from a nail always crosses a certain hole in a pegboard which is hanging loosely on the same nail. You also show that the pegboard will spin easily around a nail put through this hole. This works because the hole is in a spot called the center of gravity. The weight of the pegboard is even in all directions from this hole.

You will need an odd-shaped piece of pegboard, a string with a weight attached, a finishing nail, and a drill or awl. To make it more interesting you may want to attach a few weights of some kind to one end of the pegboard—maybe a few nuts and bolts or even a lead fishing weight.

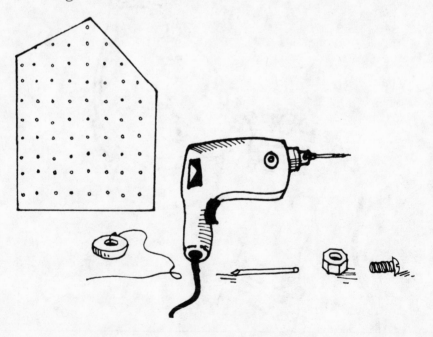

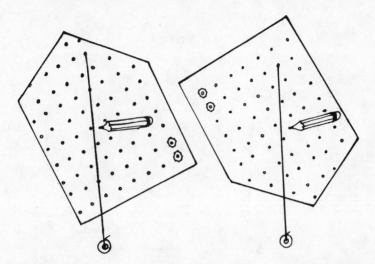

Drive the nail into a beam in the cellar, or into a handy tree, and hang the pegboard on it by any hole. Hang the string on the same nail. Draw a line on the pegboard along the string. Repeat this twice, hanging the pegboard from a different hole each time. The point where the lines cross is the center of gravity. Make a hole at this point. You may be lucky and find that this point is exactly at one of the original holes in the pegboard. You might paint the pegboard to make it more attractive, and accent the center-of-gravity hole.

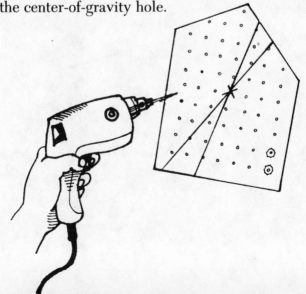

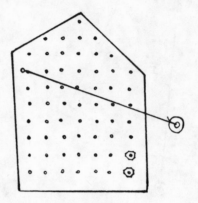

To do the trick, tell your audience that you have a magic pegboard and have drilled a hole where all the forces of nature meet. Show them that the board is not symmetrical—that is, not even all around. Show them that when you hang the board on a nail, and hang a weighted string on the same nail, the string always crosses the magic hole. Finally, hang it on a nail by the magic hole and show how you can spin the board. Show that it will not spin if it is hung from any other hole.

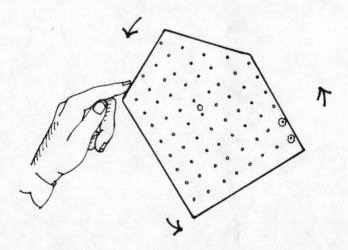

MAGIC LUNG POWER

You will need a pile of books, a plastic food bag about 11″ x 13″, some Scotch tape, and a rubber tube two or three feet long. This tube is the kind that comes with a fountain syringe or a douche bag from the drugstore. Or you can use any kind of flexible tubing you have available. Ask your mother or father.

Insert the tube into one corner of the plastic bag; fold the open end of the bag double and seal it tightly with the Scotch tape so that it is closed all the way across.

Keep this arrangement out of sight. Ask your audience if they can blow over the stack of books you have on the table by just blowing hard. When they all fail, bring out your bag-and-tube arrangement. Lay it on the table and pile the books on it. Ask for a volunteer to catch the books so they don't fall and break the bindings. Blow into the tube. The books will all fall over with very little effort on your part.

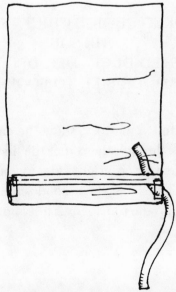

MAGIC GLASS ROD

In this trick a clear glass rod appears to turn over some words, but not others, when you look through it. You can get a glass rod from a drugstore, chemical supply house, or the bar supply section of a housewares department. Paint one tip of the rod with a dab of nail polish. This is merely to distract your audience.

Your patter can go something like this: "This magic glass rod is made from crystal mined on the continental divide of the South American Andes Mountains. On one side of the divide things flow toward the Pacific Ocean, and on the other side they flow toward the Atlantic Ocean. The molecules of this rod are therefore split so that some seem to flow in one direction and others in the opposite direction. I will demonstrate."

On separate cards carefully print *in all capital letters* the following sentences:

BOB COOKED CHOICE CHICK—FINISHED IN
THE SOUP
BILL ROASTED DUCK—DECIDED HEIDI COOK
BOB RODE BIKE TO BOOKSTORE

After you tell your story, show the cards and then let someone look through the rod at the first sentence. They will see the first phrase right side up and the second upside down. Then show the second sentence through the rod, but first flip the rod. (This is just another distraction.)

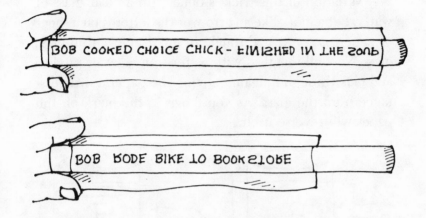

In this sentence the *first* phrase will appear upside down and the *second* right side up. Your sharp-eyed audience will have noticed that you flipped the rod and will shout that they know the secret. Let them have the rod, but show them only the third sentence. Here *every other word* will appear upside down—to their total confusion. Don't let them look at the first two sentences again. Take away the rod, telling them that their body magnetism has disarranged the molecules. Go on to another trick.

The secret, of course, is not in the glass, but in the letters. The glass turns them all upside down. But letters like O, K, and H are the same upside down, while letters like R, T, and Y are not. Make a list of all the letters that are reversible, then make as many words as you can from those letters. Then construct phrases and sentences to vary your presentation. A few more reversible words are: DOCK, DECK, HOOD, COOK, BIKE, CODE, ICE. There are many more.

A variation of this trick is done with a clear glass of water. Put a mark like an arrow or the letter R on a sheet of paper. Look at it through an empty clear thin-glass glass. Now fill the glass with water from a jar or pitcher and look through it again, moving the paper a little distance from the glass. As you move it, the mark on the paper will reverse itself.

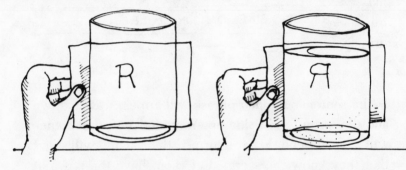

You might tell your audience that you filled the glass from a magic pitcher. If you start out with only one glassful of water in the pitcher you can then turn the pitcher upside down and say, "Look, I can turn this pitcher upside down, and no water will spill out."

MAGIC COMB

For this trick you will need a hard rubber comb; a black Ace comb from the drugstore is best. You will need a few scraps of paper and access to a water faucet.

With a pair of scissors cut out some paper dolls from a piece of paper. Make them small, 3/4″ or less. If you can't cut them out, small scraps of paper will do.

Your patter can go something like this:

"This is a magic comb that was given to me by a traveling Persian magician who was visiting here recently. He acquired it from another magician in India on his way from Iran to China. The magician's name is Ah-Kee. See, he had his name embossed on the comb—'A, C, E'; AH-KEE. It is endowed with strange magic properties. Unlike an iron magnet, which attracts only things made of iron, this comb will attract dandruff, paper, and even drinking water. Watch closely."

Lay several of the paper dolls on the table. Rub the comb vigorously against your bare arm for about twenty strokes, then hold it near the pieces of paper. They will jump up, attracted to the comb. With some practice you can even make the dolls dance on the table.

Now take your audience to the kitchen sink, and turn on the faucet so that you have the thinnest steady stream of water flowing. Again rub the comb on your arm, and hold it near the water. The stream will magically bend toward the comb!

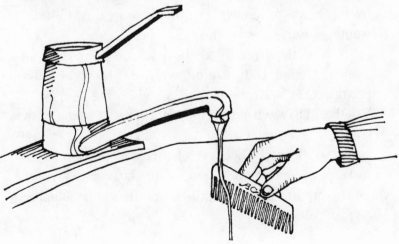

This is best done on a dry day. It may not work on a humid summer day. This trick works because the charge of static electricity in the comb is different from the charge in the bits of paper or the running water. Different charges attract each other.

MAGIC BROOMSTICK

Get a broomstick or any smooth stick four to six feet long. Mark the exact center. This will be the point where it will balance on your outstretched finger. Mark this point with a black marker so that everyone will be able to see it. You might even paint designs on the stick, or paint the two halves different colors.

Now tell your audience that it is a magic stick. Tell them that the tree from which it was made grew in a hardwood forest exactly on the Equator, where the Earth is balanced—where the northern hemisphere is balanced by the southern hemisphere. Because of this, the stick wants everything even and balanced.

To show the trick, hold the stick on your two outstretched hands as illustrated, with your hands at different distances from the center. Slowly bring your hands together. They will always meet at the exact center of the stick.

This trick works because of a law of friction. If the surfaces in contact are the same, the heavier object will exert more friction. When the broomstick is unbalanced,

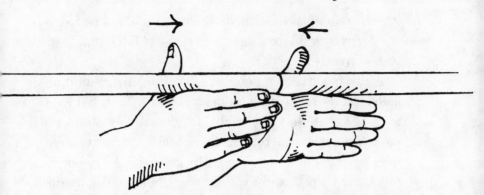

the longer portion exerts more friction and so stands still while the other hand moves in to equal the friction. Then the sides alternate in small bits until you reach the center.

MAGIC MIRROR

You will need two flat mirrors of the same size; 9″ x 9″ or larger. These flat mirrors, which are used as wall tiles, can be bought cheaply at a store or lumberyard that sells home decorating supplies. Mount each on a block of wood so that they will stand up separately and can be moved around. Also prepare a tray or board with guidelines on it so that the two mirrors can be stood so they touch each other and are exactly at right, or square, angles.

The reflection you see in a mirror is scientifically called the image. If you look into a mirror the image is backward. If you raise your right hand, the image's left hand is raised. If you hold some printing up to a mirror, it appears backward. But if you look into the magic mirror when arranged as described, the image will not be backward. If you hold up a sign that says MAGIC, it will be seen correctly.

To do your trick, let people look at the mirrors individually, so they seem to be ordinary mirrors. Then tell your audience that they are really magic mirrors, and you have the power to release their magic property. You might make it more mysterious by covering the two mirrors with a cloth while you arrange them, and mumble some incantation. Try something like, "Mirror, mirror, on the table, tell us now if you're able. Some are dull and some are bright. Are you left or are you right?"

Uncover the mirrors, and let people see the magic image. This trick works because with the double mirror arrangement, viewers see an image that has passed from one mirror to the other and then to their eyes. Thus the image is first reversed, then reversed again so that it becomes normal.

CUTTING GLASS WITH A SCISSORS

In this trick you cut a piece of ordinary glass with a pair of scissors. It is a very simple trick to perform, but you must make it look complicated to impress your audience.

Prepare a pail or pan deep enough so that when it is almost filled with water, you can get both hands under the water. You will also need several narrow strips of window glass or microscope slides, household scissors, some food colorings you disguise by putting them into dropper bottles, a bottle of tincture of iodine or Mercurochrome, some vinegar, and washing soda. Have a box of Band-Aids ready too, just for show.

You must tell your audience that you have found a secret magic formula that will soften glass so that it can be cut with ordinary scissors. To make a real impression, do one or more of the following: As you put a few drops of color into the basin of water say an incantation, like, "Mumbo-jumbo, fiddledy foo, I now put in some magic blue"; or, "This is the potion I really dread, I put in a drop of bloody red"; or, "Glass is hard, we'll make it mellow by putting in a drop of yellow." In a small jar pour a spoonful of washing soda with some vinegar, and as it bubbles up, pour it too into the basin. Then tell your audience that for safety's sake you will add a few drops of iodine, "just in case."

The important thing is to have your audience feel that you are really doing a complicated procedure.

Put several pieces of glass into the basin, and tell them it takes thirty seconds for the glass to soften up. Let them count off the seconds with you. All this hocus-pocus, of course, is just for show. The only important ingredient is the water.

Hold a piece of glass under the water and cut it with the scissors. Don't be afraid to try it—it works!

It might be a good idea to tell your audience the following: "Everyone has noticed that when you cut a thick piece of cardboard with a scissors, the part that is cut off bends away from the scissors. Because glass doesn't bend, the pieces sometimes break off." This will happen, so you must have an excuse ready.

Let some of your audience cut the glass as you did.

CRUMPLED CAN

In this trick a gallon can mysteriously crumples itself.

You will need an empty new or used rectangular can with a screw cap—the kind of can paint thinner or denatured alcohol comes in. You will also need a glass of water, a stove or other source of heat, a dry towel or potholder, and an old newspaper.

Put half a glassful of water into the can and set it on the stove to boil. While waiting for it to boil tell your story.

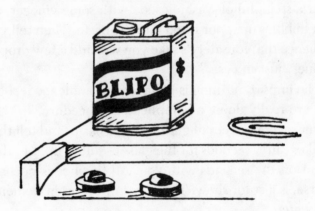

Tell your audience that you have a glass of very hard water—so hard, in fact, that when you pour it on the can it will destroy the can. If you have just done the trick of cutting glass under water (page 94), use a glass of that "magic water."

When the water in the can boils, put the cap on the can loosely, and let it boil for a minute longer. Then hold the can with the towel and tighten the cap, good and tight,

being careful not to burn yourself. Remove the can from the heat and lay it on its side on the newspaper. Pour the glass of "magic hard water" on the can. The can will crumple and bend into a weird shape.

This works because the boiling water in the can drives out all of the air. When you seal the can and pour water on it, the steam inside the can condenses, leaving a partial vacuum in the can. The air pressure outside the can, 14 pounds per square inch of area, crushes the can.

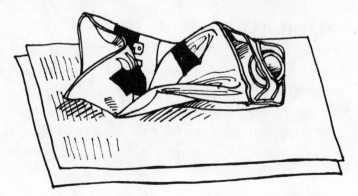

MAGIC HARBOR

This is a trick where the surface of a dish of water reacts violently when touched with a toothpick.

You will need a soup dish filled with water, some detergent, a toothpick or small plastic doll, some ground pepper, and aluminum foil or a bit of Styrofoam.

Prepare the doll or toothpick ahead of time by putting a drop of detergent on the tip. Then tell your story as you set things up.

Tell your audience that the dish represents a crowded harbor. Sprinkle pepper over the surface and tell them that the water is polluted. Drop several small balls of aluminum foil or bits of Styrofoam on the water. Call them fishing boats. You can say that the doll or the toothpick is the local Board of Health inspector. He comes to the harbor to inspect things, and touches the water. Immediately the water gets cleared up, and the boats all rush away from him.

To repeat this trick, the dish must be thoroughly rinsed so there is no detergent left in it.

MAGIC JAR #2

In this trick you will hold a jar of water upside down and the water will not fall out.

You will need a piece of stiff paper and a glass jar like the one you used in the trick described on page 69.

Hold the jar in your hand with your finger closing the hole tightly, and fill it with water. Cover the jar with the piece of paper. Hold the paper in place with your other hand and turn the jar upside down over something big enough to catch the water. Let go with the second hand. The paper will stay in place and the water will remain in the jar. Ask your audience to count out loud with you, "One . . . two . . . three." At the count of three, without letting your audience notice it, raise your finger slightly from the hole. The water will all drop out of the jar.

This trick works because with the jar upside down the only weight pressing down on the paper is the weight of the jarful of water, less than a half pound. The weight—pressure—pushing up on the paper is the entire weight of the atmosphere over the surface of the paper, about 14 pounds per square inch. When you release your finger, you have the weight of the atmosphere plus the weight of the water pushing down on the paper, so it falls away.

Miscellaneous Tricks

PAPER STRETCHER

There is an old gag of sending the new kid in the neighborhood to find a paper stretcher. Everyone knows you can't stretch paper. It will tear. In this trick we show how to get a half dollar through a hole in a piece of paper, even though the hole is only exactly as big as a quarter.

All you need in this trick is a half dollar and a piece of paper in which you cut a hole just the size of a quarter. You can use any other two coins, as long as they are obviously of different sizes.

Show the piece of paper and the coin, and ask if anyone can get the coin through the hole without tearing the paper. It might be a good idea to have several pieces of paper prepared with the hole cut in them.

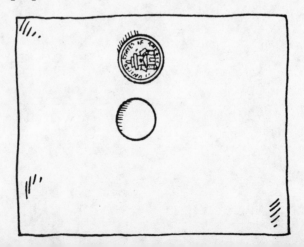

The trick is to fold the sheet of paper in half, then lay the coin inside it at the hole; if you bend the two doubled corners up toward the center, as shown in the illustration, the coin will fall through the hole.

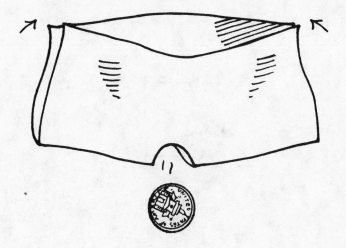

MAGIC COUNTING BLOCK

This trick shows a magic block that can answer questions. You will need a baby's wooden block with holes drilled into it and some string. The holes should be drilled at sharp angles and meet inside the block. Thread a string through the block, and tie a loop at each end.

When the string is held tightly, up and down, one end in each hand, the block will not move. When you loosen it just a tiny bit, the block will slide down the string.

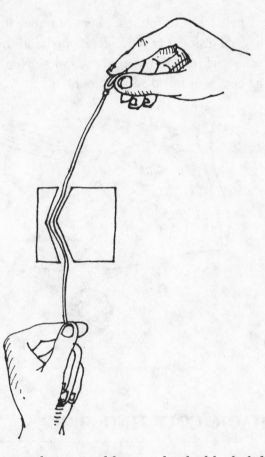

Practice with it until you are able to make the block slide or stop, but so no one can notice that you are controlling it.

Now tell your audience that you have a smart block. Not a *bright* smart block, but just an *average* smart block. It is only smart enough to count up to ten: It can do any arithmetic problem where the answer is less than ten. Ask for problems. Someone may say, "How much is ten take away seven?" For an answer, the block will make three bumps down the string.

You can also tell your audience that the block can answer questions with a yes or no—one bump for yes and two for no.

EGG MAGIC

If you are going to have several friends over for supper, prepare a hard-boiled egg for each, and put the eggs back into the refrigerator. Then when your friends are in the kitchen, bring out all the eggs, raw and cooked. Challenge them to tell which are raw and which are cooked.

Your patter can go something like this: "A man once told me of an easy way to tell if an egg is hard or raw. He said to throw it up against the ceiling. If it sticks, it's raw." After the laughs and comments you can add, "But there is a more socially acceptable way to find out. Can anyone tell me?"

The way to tell is to spin each egg. If it spins smoothly and evenly, it is cooked. If it wobbles and really won't spin, it is raw.

When Columbus returned to Spain after discovering America, his detractors said it was no great feat. Anyone could have done it. In answer Columbus asked his detractors to stand an egg on end without cracking it. Many tried, but none could do it. So Columbus showed them how, and they all said, "Oh, that's easy." "Of course it's easy after someone shows you how," Columbus replied.

Ask your friends if they can stand the egg on end.

To do it, sprinkle a little salt on the table. Now stand the egg carefully on the table in the middle of the salt, and blow away the excess salt.

MAGIC PEEPHOLE

This is a trick where you look through a hole in your hand and blow a trick whistle. You will need the cardboard cores from adding machine or cash register tapes. Ask your friendly storekeeper to save some for you. This is all you will need.

Your patter can go something like this: "This is a magic peephole. Many of you have seen a peephole in a door. If you put your eye close to it you can see outside. A keyhole that goes right through a door is also a good peephole. This is a portable peephole." Hold one up and show it. "Through it you can see the whole world, in any direction." Demonstrate by looking through it. If you get a few laughs, good. In any case go right on with your story. Tell them it *really* is a magic peephole. You can look right through your hand. It's clearer than an X ray. Here's how it works:

Just as some people are right-handed and some left-handed, so some people are right-eyed, and some left-eyed. Most people are right-eyed. We will describe the trick as if you are right-eyed. If you are left-eyed, you'll find this trick doesn't work too well. Then you just have to switch eyes.

Hold the tube to your left eye and close your right eye. Look at some object with your left eye through the tube. Now, looking steadily with your left eye, open your right eye. Slowly bring your open right hand across the right side of your face toward the end of the tube. You will find yourself looking through a round hole in your right hand.

Have everyone in the audience try it. After they are satisfied that they can look through a hole in their hands, tell them that the tube is also a magic whistle. Ask them if they can make it whistle. They will try by blowing through the tube, and get no sound at all. Tell them then, "You can only *see* through it. You mustn't *blow* through it. To make it whistle you just blow *across* the top of it, like this." Hold the bottom closed and blow a sharp blast across the open end. You will get a deep loud whistle, like a tugboat or a diesel truck.

BLIND SPOT

In this trick you show that a spot on a piece of paper can be made to disappear and reappear at will. This works because there is a spot in each of everyone's eyes that is not sensitive to light and therefore cannot see.

All you need for this trick is a piece of paper and a pen.

Make two small marks about two inches apart, like an A and a B as illustrated. Tell a person to close his left eye and look only at the A, holding the paper about a foot

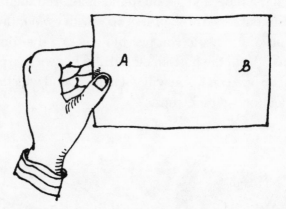

from his face. He will of course also see the B, but he must concentrate looking only at the A. Slowly bring the paper closer to his face. At some point, the B will disappear. As the paper is moved closer the B will reappear.

This can also be done with the other eye, looking at the B this time instead of the A.

You can do this on the back of your business card, which is illustrated on page 12 at the beginning of this book.

PIN IN A BALLOON

In this trick you show that you can put a pin into a balloon and the balloon will not burst. You will need balloons, pins, and some Scotch Magic Tape. This tape is best because it is invisible when put on something and smoothed carefully.

Prepare a few balloons by blowing them up and tying them shut. Then put one or two pieces of the tape on each.

To show the trick, hold up a balloon. Tell your audience that it is now filled with solid air, and that it is kept solid by the strength of your will. Tell them that you can put pins into the balloon and it will not burst. Show this by putting the pins through the Scotch tape. Now tell them that when you relax your mental power, the balloon will burst. Then put a pin into the balloon through the rubber, and of course it will burst.

MAGIC DOLLAR BILL

In this trick you show people that they are not as fast as they think they are.

You will need a table or desk, an ordinary 6½″ envelope, and, to make it interesting, a dollar bill.

Put the dollar bill into the envelope. Ask one of your audience to hold his hand on the edge of the table with his thumb and forefinger extended over the edge and held

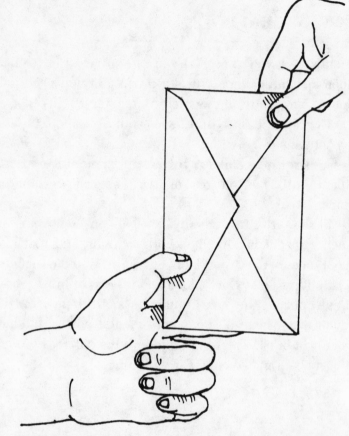

apart. Hold the envelope so that the bottom is just between his fingers. Tell him that you will let go of the
envelope, and that he is to grab it and not let it fall to the
floor. If he is successful, he may keep the dollar.

You can show how it is done by yourself. Hold the
envelope in one hand and drop it through the fingers of
your other hand. You of course will be able to grab it. But
when you drop it through another person's fingers, he can
never react fast enough to grab the envelope.

JACOB'S LADDER

This is a very tricky illusion that you must not fail to make. Your audience will be fascinated by it. The trick is quite easily made in about an hour or so. When the top slat of the ladder is folded down first one way, then the other, all the other slats seem to fall down, one at a time. It is very puzzling to watch.

You will need six to ten pieces of Masonite, each about 2½″ x 3½″, with the ends sanded somewhat round. You will also need six to ten feet of cloth tape about ½″ wide, white glue, ruler, pencil, and scissors. The directions that follow seem long and complicated, but the trick is really easy to make. You should have no trouble with it.

Each slat will have three tapes as in illustration 1: one tape in the middle, and two side tapes. Each slat should be marked with a pencil so that the tapes are evenly placed on all the slats. The side tapes can be about halfway between the middle tape and the edges of the slat.

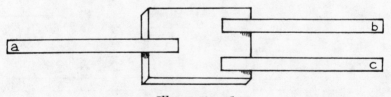

Illustration 1

Cut three pieces of tape for each slat. (The trick is even more spectacular if you use many different colors of tape.) The tapes should be at least 2″ longer than the slats. A drop of glue should hold them in place.

Illustration 2

Lay the first slat on the table with the tapes on the bottom as in illustration no. 2. Fold the three tapes up and over so it looks like illustration no. 3. Lay the second slat on top of this with its tapes on the bottom as with the first slat. It should now look like illustration no. 4. Pull tapes a, b, and c so they are snug, fold them up and over the second slat and glue them in place as in illustration no. 5.

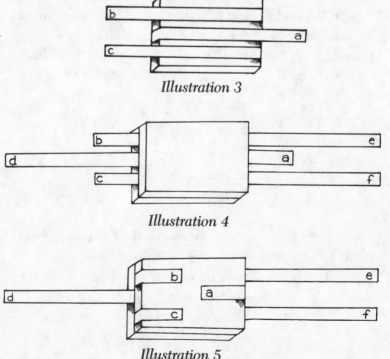

Illustration 3

Illustration 4

Illustration 5

Keep repeating this procedure to complete the ladder. The last slat will not have any of its own tapes.

The completed ladder will look like illustration 6. Put it aside over night to allow the glue to harden.

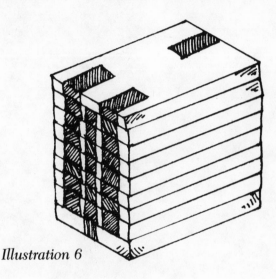

Illustration 6

To operate the trick, hold it by the top slat and let the rest hang down. Fold slat 1 all the way over and slat 2 will fall away. All the rest of the slats will follow. Then fold slat 1 all the way over in the opposite direction. All the slats will again fall away all the way down the line. Keep repeating this, first to one side, then the other.

This is really a very ancient toy invented by the Chinese. You can tell a story that it was invented by your ancient Chinese ancestors, and passed down through the generations as a family secret all the way to you.

WHERE TO FIND THE CHEMICALS AND INGREDIENTS USED IN THESE TRICKS

Chemicals and other items needed for the various tricks are listed below in alphabetical order, with synonyms and sources of supply. Drugstores are one source. The older, smaller stores would be more likely to have the chemicals than the newer super stores. If you have a high school or college in your town, a friendly chemistry instructor may be able to give you small amounts of chemicals you may find inconvenient to get elsewhere. Some toy stores carry a big variety of chemicals to replace those available in the chemistry sets they sell.

In the following list the easiest source of supply is abbreviated following the name of the chemical, as follows: DS = drugstore; M = food market; MO = mail order. A list of mail-order sources is on page 116.

Ammonia, clear   M
Ammonia solution   See page 116
Alcohol = 70% ethyl rubbing alcohol   DS
Aluminum foil   M
Baby oil   DS, M
Baking soda = Sodium Bicarbonate   DS, M
Boric acid   DS
Cabbage, red   M
Cabbage water   See page 116
Candle   M

Copper Sulfate = blue stone = blue vitriol   DS, MO,
   hardware store, or a pool supply business
Copper sulfate solution   See page 116
Dropper bottle   DS; or a used nose drop bottle
Epsom salts = magnesium sulfate   DS
Ethyl alcohol   See Alcohol
Ex-Lax ᴅDS
Feen-A-Mint   DS
Ferric chloride   DS, MO
Hypo = sodium thiosulfate = sodium hyposulfite   DS,
   photo supply store, MO
Iodine = tincture of iodine   DS; see also page 116
Iron filings   MO or see page 116.
Magnesium sulfate   see epsom salts
Mercurochrome   DS
Methanol = methyl alcohol   DS, MO
Methyl alcohol   See Methanol
Mineral oil   DS
Mineral spirits = subturps = paint thinner   Hardware
   store, paint store
Oxalic acid   DS, hardware store
Paint thinner   See Mineral spirits
Phenolphthalein solution   See page 116
Potassium nitrate = saltpeter   DS, MO
Q-tips (or any brand of cotton-tipped stick)   DS, M
Red cabbage   M
Rubbing alcohol   See Alcohol
Saltpeter   See Potassium nitrate
Sodium bicarbonate   See baking soda
Sodium carbonate = washing soda   M

Sodium hyposulfite   See Hypo
Sodium thiosulfate   See Hypo
Subturps   See Mineral Spirits
Steel wool   M, hardware store
Sterno (canned heat)   DS, M, hardware store, camping
    supply store
Tannin = tannic acid   DS, MO
Turmeric   M (spice shelf)
Turmeric solution   See page 116
Tincture of iodine   See Iodine
Washing soda   See sodium carbonate

SOME MAIL-ORDER SOURCES
OF CHEMICALS

Gabriel Industries, Inc.
P.O. Box 980
Hagerstown, MD 21740

Natural Science Industries
51-17 Rockaway Beach Blvd.
Far Rockaway, NY 11691

Perfect Parts Co.
1 North Haven Street
Baltimore, MD 21224

MAKING AND USING
CERTAIN INGREDIENTS

AMMONIA SOLUTION—Use clear, not sudsing, ammonia from the market. For all the tricks calling for ammonia, mix it half and half with water.

CABBAGE WATER—Get a small head of red cabbage at the market. Cut up half of it into smaller pieces and put it into a saucepan. Cover it with water and bring it to a boil. Shut off the heat, and pour the liquid into a jar through a strainer. You will have a jarful of purple liquid. Keep this in the refrigerator. Put a label on it, "Cabbage Water."

To concentrate this cabbage water, put it into a saucepan and allow it to boil away until there is only a very little left, maybe only half a juice glassful. Keep this in a jar in the refrigerator. Label it, "Conc. Cabbage Water."

IODINE, TINCTURE OF—This will stain anything you spill it on, so you must be careful how you handle it. Always work with it on a thick layer of old newspaper. Always pour it as shown in the illustration. The iodine will flow

down the applicator attached to the cap and go exactly where you want it. This way, you will not spill any, nor will any run down the side of the bottle.

IRON FILINGS—These can easily be made just by rubbing together two pieces of dry steel wool without soap and catching the tiny pieces on a piece of paper.

MAGNETS—Small straight magnets can be purchased in toy, craft, or hobby shops. The round ring magnets, called ceramic round magnets, can be obtained in stores that sell electronic supplies. A good size is 1⅛″. You can get these at Radio Shack stores, of which there are several thousand all around the country. Their catalogue number is 64-1885.

PHENOLPHTHALEIN SOLUTION—From the drugstore, get a small package of any laxative pill that contains phenolphthalein. These include Ex-Lax, Feen-A-Mint, Es-potabs, Alophen. With a fork, mash one or two pieces in a saucer with some rubbing alcohol. Let it settle for a minute, pick up the liquid with the dropper, and transfer it to the dropper bottle.

STYROFOAM—You can get small pieces of styrofoam by breaking off pieces from an egg carton or a white tray of the kind the meat department of a supermarket uses for packaging.

TURMERIC SOLUTION—Turmeric is a spice which you will find on the spice shelf of the market. To make the solution, sprinkle a little into a small glass or saucer and add a little alcohol—a tablespoonful or so. Swish it around for a few seconds. That's all. It is ready to use.

INDEX

Addition tricks, 17-19

Blind spot trick, 106
Boat trick, 65-66
Box illusions, 76-78, 81
Broomstick trick, 92-93

Calendar trick, 15-17
Can crumpling trick, 96-97
Candle trick, 42-43
Checkers trick, 50-51
Chemicals and other ingredients, 113-19; mail order sources, 116; making and using, 117-19
Chemistry tricks, 33-49
Circle trick, 30-31
Coin tricks, 50-52
Colored water trick, 44-45
Comb trick, 90-92
Corinth Canal illusion, 78
Counting blocks trick, 101-03
Crumpled can trick, 96-97
Cutting glass with scissors trick, 94-95

Deep purple magic, 37
Disappearing squares and lines, 25-32
Dollar bill trick, 107-08

Egg tricks, 103-04
Energetic coins, 50

Fire trick, 43-44
Flying ping-pong ball, 82-83

Glass cutting with scissors trick, 94-95
Glass rod trick, 88-90
Green flame magic, 48-49

Helicopter (paper) trick, 57-58
Hexagon figure tricks, 32, 76
Hex and double hex, 61-64

Impossible fork illusion, 79
Inertia tricks, 50-52
Ink magic, 47

Jacob's ladder trick, 109-11

Jars, tricks with, 51, 70-71, 98-99

Ketchup magic, 45-47

Lazy jar trick, 51
Lines, tricks and illusions, 25-32, 72-81
Long and short lines illusion, 73

Magic addition boxes, 17-19
Magic boat, 65-66
Magic boomerang illusion, 74-76
Magic box illusion, 76-78
Magic broomstick, 92-93
Magic candle trick, 42-43
Magic comb, 90-92
Magic counting block, 101-03
Magic dollar bill trick, 107-08
Magic envelope, 30-31
Magic flower, 34-36
Magic glass rod, 88-90
Magic green flame, 48-49
Magic harbor trick, 98
Magic hexagon, 32, 76
Magic ink, 47
Magic jar tricks, 70-71, 98-99
Magic ketchup, 45-47
Magic lung power, 87
Magic mirror, 93-94

Magic numbers, 21-24
Magic paper doorway, 55-57
Magic peephole, 104-05
Magic pegboard, 84-86
Magic pile of boxes, 81
Magic rectangle, 29-30
Magic rings, 67-69
Magic squares, 13-19, 25-29
Magic staircase illusion, 80
Magic star trick, 53-55
Magic tea glass, 38
Magic triangle, 29
Magic wet fire, 43-44
Magnets, tricks with, 65-71
Mathematics tricks, 13-24
Mirror trick, 93-94
Monster doll trick, 58-60

Number tricks, 13-24

Optical illusions, 72-81

Paper cutting tricks, 53-64
Paper stretcher trick, 100-01
Peephole trick, 104-05
Pegboard trick, 84-86
Physics tricks, 82-99
Ping-pong ball trick, 82-83
Pin in a balloon trick, 107
Potato spearing trick, 51

Rectangle trick, 29-30
Ring magnet trick, 67-69

Secret writing, 41-43
Squares, tricks with,13-19, 25-29
Staircase illusion, 80
Subtraction trick, 19-20

Tea into water trick, 38
Tower of discs trick, 50-51

Triangle trick, 29
Tunnel flip-flop, 72-73

Water tricks, 38, 44-45, 90, 98
Witch's dust trick, 38-40
Writing magic, 41-43

ABOUT THE AUTHOR

Nathan Shalit grew up in Newark, New Jersey. He graduated from Rutgers University College of Pharmacy and is a community pharmacist in Morristown, New Jersey. Author of the prize-winning book of chemical experiments, *Cup and Saucer Chemistry,* he frequently gives chemistry demonstrations at local elementary and junior high schools.

ABOUT THE ILLUSTRATOR

Helen Cerra Ulan is a free-lance illustrator who lives in Fairfax, Virginia.